VIEWS FROM ALONG THE MIDDLE WAY

Views from along the Middle Way

poems by

Thomas Centolella

COPPER CANYON PRESS

Cover art: *Mount Fuji and Seashore at Miho No Matsubara,*
Kano Tanyū (1602–1674), ASIAN ART MUSEUM OF SAN FRANCISCO,
The Avery Brundage Collection, Chong-Moon Lee Center for
Asian Art and Culture, B63 D7A, det.

Copper Canyon Press is in residence under the auspices of
the Centrum Foundation at Fort Worden State Park in
Port Townsend, Washington. Centrum sponsors artist residencies,
education workshops for Washington State students and teachers,
blues, jazz, and fiddle tunes festivals, classical music performances,
and The Port Townsend Writers' Conference.

Library of Congress Cataloging-in-Publication Data

Centolella, Thomas.
    Views from along the middle way : poems / by Thomas Centolella.
        p.   cm.
    Includes bibliographical references.
    ISBN 9781556591617 (paper)
    1. Love poetry, American.   1. Title.
PS3553.E65 V54 2002
811'.54—dc21

                                                2001006506

COPPER CANYON PRESS
Post Office Box 271
Port Townsend, Washington 98368
www.coppercanyonpress.org

ACKNOWLEDGMENTS

My gratitude to the editors of *Barnabe Mountain Review*, *Runes*,
and *The Marin Poetry Center Anthology, Volume Four*, where some
of these poems first appeared.

My appreciation to the Lannan Foundation for a Writer's Residency.

And my deep thanks to Molly Giles and Brenda Hillman
for their moral support.

CONTENTS

For all the great teachers:

Nadine Macdonald, Philip Booth, Carl Dennis, Denise Levertov, and Robert Aitken. You helped me get this far. Thank you.

In the middle of the journey of our life
I came to myself in a dark wood
Where the true way was lost to me.

· Dante, *Inferno*

In the midst of this world
we stroll along the roof of hell
gawking at flowers

· Issa

VIEWS FROM ALONG THE MIDDLE WAY

VIEW #1: WEST

for Burr Overstreet

"The heart" this, "the heart" that —
I need something more capacious and durable,
I need desert, I need ocean, I need a range
of mountains, a cordillera with a valley
sloping off to either side, green and supernal,
as far as the eye can reach
until the next range, the next valley...

Cholla, coyote, scampering quail
with their silly plume curling out
of each head like a party favor —
yes, and throw in the skitter
of sandpipers across the wet littoral,
the cuneiform scribble their feet leave behind —

the same text that loomed, untranslatable,
over the highway by the Great Divide,
a giant Sumerian tablet of granite
dusted with snow. (Was it a record
of all the days behind us
and before us? I couldn't decipher
one character, and didn't need to know.)

Crouched over the mountain creek so clear
I had to dip my fingers in it
to make sure it was there,
I didn't want to leave —
and knew I had to leave.

Starting out, my heart
was only human size. So how
did this world come to fit
so beautifully into it?

3

It was just one task to recover the taken-for-granted.
There were others. Such as: simply recover.

And then? And then consider
there's no time off for good behavior,

that the city was a carnival of incandescent streets
but also a dim labyrinth, that the beloved bridge

connecting two wonders of solid ground
provided as well a jumping-off point

for those who had lost heart.
That some roads, no matter how far

they take you, will double back.
And then? And then consult the window

for weather. Put on some clothes
and good intentions. Begin again.

View #8

He then who does not wish to sink in the
wretchedness of the finite is constrained,
in the deepest sense, to assault the infinite.

KIERKEGAARD

It's late and you don't know
if you're up for the infinite.
Won't a long walk do as well?
A cold night, very late,
and very still. You feel how
it's almost emptier with you
than without you.
Suddenly a gust,
a clatter down the street,
something used up
and discarded, but which won't go away
that easily. Your heart
picks up the pace, your feet
hurry in the opposite direction,
though you have no idea
where you're going.
That's the point. To have
no idea at all. To feel
and not to think.
The wind kicks up,
cumuli rolling in,
the dim stars disappearing.
One last bright window
goes dark. It's time:
there is someone else turning
their light out
whose only refuge from the finite
is the thought of you
moving through the ordinary
hours, distant
as an unnamed moon

whose only hope for discovery
is in the eye of their mind.
Meanwhile, you're advancing through
the same deep space
planets inhabit. And you'll continue
your modest assault on the infinite
into sleep, its tree-lined road
through open country. Sometimes
the world is merely
empty, except for its refuse,
and goes nowhere, like a
cul-de-sac. And sometimes
it's empty but wide open,
the fruitless winter vines
dreaming of a vintage season.
You don't need anything
that isn't yours to keep going.
If someone is holding you
inside themselves
the way you're learning
to hold them, so much
the better. Sometimes
there is no difference
between a mind and a mind,
a heart and a heart, a mind
and a heart. Sometimes
the world won't move
unless you move.
Won't hold its course
unless you show it how.
And sometimes, the world holds
the two of you in one moment
and whispers: *Yes. Now.*

Beach sand in the bed,
all night we rubbed against it —
new moon our dark pearl

Two for the Fire

1. Late Spring

The old wooden witch they call Winter in the old country,
paraded through the cobbled streets
to the whistles and shrieks of an adoring throng,
all eyes on her all the way to the bonfire
(originally, a *bone fire*) — I was tempted
but passed on the chance to think
her hair was as long as yours,
her stick limbs as thin as your living
bones, draped in a lacy nothing...

But then, held aloft, exalted in her high
reign above the frenzy of women and men,
and children permitted to play at being women and men,
spirits and small explosives at their disposal,
she began to turn from side to side —
not under her own power, of course,
she was being turned — and I was helpless
to keep from thinking of how you would dance
for your rapt, gratifying audience
of one: after midnight, the wine drunk,
the candles lit, delirious wail
of an ancient reed, the bass line and drum
a euphoric thrum not so much heard as felt,
moving you to shed one layer after another,
the attention you craved and I gladly gave
moving you to reenact the provocative ways
I had touched you, and would touch you again —
a ritual you would come to call "healing" —
until I believed there was no intimacy
we could not, in our time, approach
and enter — just as winter, lingering as it was,
inexorable-seeming, relented at last
to the felicities of March: the sun magnanimous,

the pale poppies revealing their secrets,
your pale legs revealing your secrets,
brief season of opening...

The evil queen of winter sits on a throne
designed for burning. Her loyal subjects have gone
eerily quiet. Long flames scorch everything pale
and beyond the pale. The silver streak
in her dark hair. The cold hands. The face,
impassive as ice. And the heart —
if a heart were there.

2. *Eros and Agape*

What you would use
to cross your most dangerous chasm,
praying along the way
a fearless traveler might join you —
and when one did, how high
you'd get (or so you'd say),
an astonishing spasm
engendered more by anguish than joy,
a long-in-coming cry
to wake the dead and worry
the neighbors: the wail of one lost
and then found, who would not be
abandoned — what you used to cross
your most dangerous chasm,
and reaching open ground, then a secret path
where fellow traveler couldn't find you,
what you dismissed out of hand
and heart, what you left
burning behind you.

WATER

Inviting to my touch, but cool at first.
Then warmer the longer I held you.

Left to yourself: fluent in fits and starts.
Around every bend, impedimenta.

But gathering yourself in sun, in shade, a pool
of having-at-last-nothing-to-do,

you were the gladness that drew me in,
that I was glad to slip into,

element to which I best corresponded.
A human being, they say, is nearly all water —

which might explain why the more I tried
to hold you, the less of you remained.

VIEW #20: NORTH

So far north
they talk of temperature
in December
not in "minus" degrees
but "negative": "It's negative three
right now — not bad —
but tonight it'll hit
negative thirty"

A visitor from Tennessee
thought he could outrun
the cold crystallizing
in his Southern lungs

He was wrong

but lived to never make
that mistake again

So far north the sun
when there is sun
barely skims the horizon
from one end of the day
to the other

And in the sameness
of dim hours I couldn't name
snatches of song
would appear to me

"When the night comes
You're already dreaming
But you don't see
What's written in the sky
You can have any answer I've got
But you don't ask me why"

And one night
as if from a dream
in which your hidden wishes
are considered worthy
someone's warm breath
delivering the message

"It'll be interesting
to see how the world
will work things out"

Being there was simple —
horizontal thoughts
vertical feelings

Even waiting
for aurora borealis
to show itself
and waiting   and waiting
I could believe we belonged
to joy

And as for the photographer who said
it takes a lot of patience
some nights nothing happens
the energy builds up
slowly

but when the sky erupts
it's true magic
intense displays

they usually don't last
too long —

as for him
as for us
he wasn't wrong

VIEW #27: INSPIRATION POINT

Was it the desert's
thin air? The higher we climbed
the deeper the silence

∽

Dark soul and dark soul —
still, the gorgeous light followed
loyal as a dog

∽

Outcrop like a cloud —
and two uncertain gods, floating
on creation's edge

∽

Dewdrops, finger-teased
from the tiniest crevice,
and we — crazed, breathless

∽

In a thicket we
stripped — the more naked, the more
illuminated

∽

Great inspiration,
you were cruel to touch us
as if you cared

DEVOTIONAL

Sandalwood incense in the street again.
Just past the corner store, another open door:
a dim room, an altar on a bureau,

candles in red glass, oranges and flowers,
a wedding day in black and white, the young
couple smiling like wartime heroes.

And jade Buddha, also smiling, shrunk
to the size of a pear — not a god but a guide
through the ten thousand sorrows —

while the old woman watches TV from a kitchen chair.
Scene after scene from the country left behind.
She rubs her hands slowly — perhaps an exotic prayer

for the man beside her in a hospital bed,
his eyes closed to the blue room
that surrounds him like the sky of a dying planet.

Incense drifts, misty as a nebula.
Who knows how remote he is, what distant star
he is orbiting that no one can name?

And who knows how she has managed
to follow, bright moon to his absence
of thought and emotion, a devotion

irresistible as gravity, no matter
how bad the hand that's dealt: a tenacious,
yet tender, holding to the difficult

day and night, night and day —
while every other living thing, loving
or not, loosens its grip, slips away.

In the mad late-day rush to the celebrated
bridge, along Doyle Drive where cars
take the concrete turn at 45, a dark
figure in the early dark moves slowly between
the stream of metal and the still stone —
and I don't mean on the sidewalk side —
the darkness that moves in a human form
and abides by no law except its own.

⁓

A Sunday stroll on our favorite beach —
the one that begins with houses high on their privileged cliff
and reaches out to the bridge. Sun vanishing
and with it the heat, the nude sunbathers long gone,
the long-pole fishermen gone, the couples with their broods,
the loners and their antic dogs. We had our heavy sweaters on
and headed for the rocks. And there he was:
lying on his belly, motorcycle jacket, casually
reading a paperback — and from the waist down, stark naked.
Fat rump. Legs plump and hairless, deliberately splayed,
it seemed, to showcase his equally depilated balls.
And the small chain, looping out of shadow to the shock
of one pink testicle, as if on a door
he was daring anyone to unlock.

⁓

The rains interminable, the rivers risen
beyond their banks, and someone
with a microphone in Monterey
asks a man outside a market
called La Esperanza what he's managed
to salvage. A man who never expected
he would have anything to say
to a million strangers — and who says,

without drama, a word as devastating
as any act of God: *Nada.*

~

She's been around for years.
A wisp of flesh over a wisp of bone.
Mismatched eyes above the metal grid
that keeps her gappy teeth in place.
Sores punctuating her skin, some shiny,
some dull, like the dreaded pennies
that keep popping up. She begs
by invoking the name of a notorious disease
that would have had to do her in a long time ago.
Sometimes she offers a "Sir" or "Ma'am"
but never takes "no" for an answer, spitting
a word as dirty as her outstretched hand.
Sometimes what might be a tear
seeps into her eye — maybe only
the sharp wind she's made to stand in.
She is everything we fear,
streetcorner prophet of doom
disguised as a beleaguered beggar.
She is everywhere we turn —
and won't be leaving anytime soon.

~

He was the zeitgeist writ small: manic,
driven, self-directed without direction,
except for the narrow purposes of the self.
In the family snapshots he's Harpo Marx
in pajamas: curly-haired master of mischief
at the age of six. And older, a local star, shooting
from the playgrounds to the big-time
ballparks. The impressive stats, the trophies,
the newspaper photographs — not a clue

to the disaster waiting down the road:
gambling debts, a drug deal gone wrong,
his "employers" duct-taping his mouth,
hog-tying him to a chair — you can guess the rest.
Who says we're more than flesh and blood?
His smothered screams — not of a man, exactly,
nor even a woman, but an animal,
forced into the terrible knowledge
that it is human, all too human.

Nothing escaped me, my blessing and my curse.
Smudge of hand grease on the underground ticket machine.
Well-tanned ponytailed man, pissing against a mailbox.
A woman nursing her newborn against a downtown monolith,
complexion wan, fingers ringless. Something burning
in the expensive bistro, though no one else could detect it.

And the schoolgirl near The House of Pain —
which is what the vice cops call the local drug joint —
her eyes as splendid to behold as the pustules on her face were horrible,
who asked me sotto voce if I was looking for a "date" —
her textbooks pressed to the white blouse
that held the dim light of her breasts.

And when the commuter bus turned onto the bridge,
not far from the oil slick that ranged over the bay
like the shadow of an avenging angel,
don't you think I noticed the heavy yellow phone
with the sign: EMERGENCY SERVICES AND CRISIS COUNSELING?

Maybe I wanted to die, the world seemed so intent
on running itself down, so willfully
decrepit, so destitute of glory.

Not the world itself
but how we wasted it.

&

Because I had run out of resources
and what good news there was
was not good enough, and my allies
were chin-deep in their own emotional
negotiations, I went to see the oracle.

And the oracle said, not unkindly:
"Work it out for yourself. Give it
some time. Be diligent."

&

Every morning I had to remind myself:
I am a responsible, devoted particle of the galaxy.
I am a run of intelligence.
I am a petroglyph hiding out from the garish glare of culture.

But every evening, the same old story:
I was a comet blazing through time, the loneliness was crushing.
I was what followed the "greater than" sign that followed ignorance.
I was standing in one spot while the world darkened all around me.

&

When nothing else sustained me, I relied on peaches.
It sounds silly, but they taught me patience.
You have to wait until they ripen, then study their colors:
the scarlet flare of humiliation, secret desire's
deeper red, a little sundown afterglow.
Hungry as I was, broke as I was,
I wouldn't eat them even then,
they taught me so well to wait.

It was enough to hold them to my nose
and sniff, to think of how they held
their succulence — without complaint —
and would yield it without complication.
Think of how they were made
to be eaten: slowly. With absurd consideration.
With a satisfaction so disturbingly rare
its absence was an ache.

❧

I'm a radio,
my frequencies are multiple
and, at a touch, mutable.

At times I'm so remote
from the source
of transmission, I drift
from one era to another —

Bach cantata morphing
into a Santana riff —

or I drift
from voice to impassioned voice,
the pimps of a venal planet
who pitch everything
from motor oil to the ideal mate
in tones of equal earnestness.

I'm a receiver
whose wavelengths attenuate,
I don't know how far I can go
without losing touch for good.

But I do know this:
it's becoming easier and easier
to turn me off, to turn
myself off, to turn...

∽

What if the silhouette along Doyle Drive,
dragging its ragged animus at the edge
of breakneck traffic, is not anyone
slogging through their thirties or forties

but a thirteen-year-old year old genius
of rejection — jilted by Mom
or math teacher, classmate
or crush — and his brethren

are everywhere, even
in the backwaters of the Bible Belt,
an unofficial militia
of pissed-off pubescents

with access to an arsenal
(Dad's or Granddad's, either will do),
someone taught expertly
how to shoot, clad

in jungle khaki and Scripture
on his lips — what if
revenge opened fire
on your community, and was taken

into custody, and the world cried
to put him away — if not down — and you

his incredulous neighbor, dispirited teacher,
fatally wounded father, fatally wounded mother...

꒰

After the power surge blacked out
the better part of five states,
the systems manager explained:
"We're all on the same power grid
and you cannot affect one part of the system
without affecting all the other parts."

But when asked what caused
the surge itself, all he could say was:
"The electrons flow wherever..."

꒰

You can be a radio, yes,
but at times a satellite as well,
deployed expertly into orbit,
the views from the magnetosphere
magnificent, swirling
whites of weather,
the radiant blues
of ocean — all the ceaseless

flux of complex systems —

and you above it all,
circling without effort,
taking in whatever is given
and giving it back

without effort, without care —

beautiful, remote, oblivious
disseminator of everything
that could possibly matter

and does not matter.

☙

Because the one I had come to trust
betrayed that trust, and I was riven
between anger (protection)
and compassion (connection),
I went to see the oracle.

And the oracle said:
"Not to laugh, not to lament,
not to curse, but to understand.
If you can help others, then help them.
If you cannot, at least refrain from harm."

☙

How many times have I listened to the victims
of some natural disaster tell their story
and thought: Why are these people *smiling?*
Like the "cliff dweller" on Pacifica's coastal bluff.
In the eighth week of rain they red-tagged his house.
His backyard high above the beach
had already crumbled down to it.
Now El Niño was gnawing at his porch.
The sun hadn't been seen in months.
He pointed down to his neighbor's debris,
driftwood deluxe, a new kind of sea wrack
or sea wreck. "See that?" He pointed down,
he chuckled. "That's the sundeck."

☙

Because no one is not given to suffering,
each of us invents.

The fourteen-year-old with Nubian nosering, smacked-around,
taciturn, dreams "a machine
that says what you're really feeling."

The seventy-year-old at the health center,
who can retrieve nothing from the day before,
asserts with a smile, "This is the first day
I've been alive."

The glum beauty who has lost all sense
of beauty, or its worth, or the reason
for her desperation, has taken to photographing
herself, in the nude. "Tomorrow," she laughs,
"I'm getting a tattoo: two snakes curling
around each other."

And I, who must invent hope, I think:
sign of the healer.

∽

When nothing else sustained me, I relied on music.
Reggae, blues, zydeco, chant, folk rock, highlife, samba,
bebop, hip-hop, acid house, trance, raga, salsa, a cappella...
Jobim's "Desafinado" and Veloso's "Terra." The Marley Man's
"No Woman No Cry." Stevie Ray caught in a "Crossfire,"
Thelonious noodling through "Well, You Needn't."

And King Sunny Adé: *Synchro   Synchro   Synchro Sys-tem*

∽

Cold night at the hot springs
a couple of us floated volunteers

25

faceup to the stars, closed their eyes,
then commandeered their bodies
through a cosmic drift
while someone chanted
Sappho in Greek: "Evening comes
bringing all things
which the bright dawn
has scattered...." And someone
floating said it felt old
as eons, like a mystery rite,
like a blessing for the newborn,
and someone else joked
about being born again —
the pool, after all, was round
and warm as a womb
and Sappho was singing:
"You bring the lamb,
you bring the goat,
you bring the child
to its mother" — and the floater
said it felt somehow like
an epiphany, turning slowly
as the cosmos turned, elated...
But then this other voice,
the youngest among us — arrogant
or bitter, it wasn't clear — saying
epiphanies were overrated.

∽

Because peaches are, after all, only peaches
and not patience, I went to see the oracle.
And the oracle said: "Go for a walk.
Go home. Sit with it."

∽

RIFT ZONE said the sign at the trailhead.
But I was sick of the status quo.
In the dusty windshield I drew a circle,
installed a capital R, then a slash — a logo
against the deep-down slide and shift,
old mischief saying it had had enough,
though where it came from, how...

Because it was a pleasure,
unexpected but not unfamiliar,
I chose to think of it as a gift.

∽

Male of the species
Homo sapiens, age
five months, butt-naked
on a bed, upper body
supported by the arms
in the manner of The Cobra,
plump thighs and rump and head,
a chubby Buddha baby,
or maybe Bacchus, the smile
of easy mirth, drunken
revelry, already he's forgotten
the noose at birth
around his neck,
and hasn't yet learned
the nature of pain,
unpredictable, imminent,
inflicted often by others
of his own kind,
arriving in many guises,
not the least of which
are an unaccountable loneliness,

cruel remarks, intentional
or not, resonating
throughout his days, violent
acts against his person
he will carry in the cells
beneath his skin, deftly
embedded with the generations
that precede him, and will
succeed him, or possibly
not, given the factors
neither he nor anyone
can foresee, though here
and now he is delighted
to be the center
of time's attention,
his two toy animals,
button-eyed dog
and smiling pony, at his side
like guardian spirits,
he has plenty of time
and doesn't have long
to come to know
who is for him and who
against him, who will cherish
his trust or trash it, who
will teach him how to be
faithful and/or perfidious,
plenty of time, and no time
at all for the charming
delusions to play themselves
out, for the enervating
Sunday afternoons, lying
bellydown like a beached seal,
the heartless waiting
for a few human words

to make all the difference,
or a look or a gesture, the lack
of which will teach him
limits, his own and those
of others, and something else
as central but beyond
his ken: how he can pick up
a loaded gun, aim at what
he can't accept,
swallow hard,
put it down.

∽

When nothing else sustained me, I relied on my favorite tales.
Two friends, convicted of a crime, are sentenced
to walking a tightrope over a windy abyss.
They draw straws to see who will go first.
The first one, not without difficulty, makes it
to the other side. The second one, already in a sweat
before he's even begun, calls out: "My friend,
how did you do it? What's the secret?"
And the first one calls back: "All I know is
whenever I started drifting to one side
I leaned toward the other."

∽

Because pain moved through the chronicle
of years like a circle turning to complete itself,
but never quite connecting (a spiral, then,
by turns ascending and descending),
I went to see the oracle.

And the oracle said:
"We say the sun rises, the night falls —
when everything is merely turning

and turning. The hero will be the one
who endures the pain
without passing it on."

&

Maybe I was fed up with ambition's drift
and attrition's latest hard-luck story.
The Pacific, the Peaceful One,
lived up to its name from the edge of the cliff,
beauty's open invitation: birth and death
and desire swelling its lovely spume between the two.

Maybe I was so weary it was time to leave.
Then others started to exit for me.
When his doctor gave up chemo for morphine
Robert came right out and said, "It won't be
long now." But he was still cracking wise,
he was still *here,* I insisted. "Okay," he laughed,
"so I'll equivocate my way through each day,"
as if he were doing me a favor, hanging on
so I wouldn't feel so alone — and he
just days away from the ultimate unknown.

&

When nothing escapes you, when everything fails
to surprise, when you can see it all coming
because of all the times it has appeared before,
it must be the sweetest relief to yield
to the unknown. For all the ghosts
said to haunt the living, they don't
number nearly as many
as those who don't bother to return.

I was walking back from Baker Beach,
a crescent moon of sand
with the bridge at one end,
where, for an hour or two, the past and the future
were beside the point, where desire
was just so much ebb and flow, and hope
a translucent fish too little to keep.

I was walking back and the hilly streets
rolled like waves, peaks
and valleys, the rise and fall and rise
of the elemental, the great overriding order
from which, for reasons unknown to me,
I had been cut loose... And I couldn't stop

walking — I can't explain it —
inside the day was this other day
that didn't want to end, didn't want me
to disappear — my blessing and my curse —
so I kept walking, and soon
the storefronts and the houses revealed a patina
like gold leaf, the shabby stacks of apartments
glistening like a honeycomb, and every face I passed
owned a Mediterranean glow — all of which I knew

was only the low sun up to its old tricks,
the sun that knew everything there is to know
about rising and falling: The illusion. And the magnificence.

Those who came before us
had a father who made sure
they washed behind the knees
and did not want for chocolate,
or a father whose breath was
something hot and rotten,
whose nose bled all over
his potatoes and meat.
Those who came before us
had a mother more admired
by other children than by her own,
or a mother so determined to be
worthy of the name, she inspired
forgiveness, if not greatness.
Many of those before us
sat long into the night
before a mesmerizing play
of shadow and light, though
many others consulted
the texts available. And some were
so eager for fortune or advice
they were content to read the stars,
steaming entrails, the random
landing of coins. They were a vexed
and lonely and desperate bunch,
the ones who came before us.
Did I mention that often
they didn't know where
they were going? Often they didn't
know where they were going.
The lucky few among them
arrived somewhere useful anyway,
while the cursed were too knowing
to trust the smallest gift
intrinsic to any given moment.

These too were givens for the ones
before us: climate, terrain, gravity.
Hunger pangs of two kinds. Bodies
susceptible to pleasure and pain,
much of it not explicable.
Breath. Electricity. Foreknowledge
of death. Many knew too well
the dolor of doing nothing, many
the despair of their best efforts
not being good enough. Some
were masters at pretending
they didn't care when disappointment
slipped in, or slights, or even more
flagrant demeanings. For some of those
before us, meaning itself
was held in the highest esteem
but too enormous to be held
to any one reading. Of those
before us, not enough allowed
for their influence
on those who would follow,
not enough chose to see
that far. In the long run
it wouldn't matter. The strong
sun rose over those before us,
the strong sun left them behind.
And here we are.

LOOP

Sitting one morning
as in a movie theater, watching
the film play out
a familiar arc:
loneliness, attraction,
projection, inspiration,
seduction, adoration,
seduction, deception,
acrimony, invective,
all of which
had me transfixed —
until repetition kicked in,
especially the brutal scenes
at the end, and I started
to rise from my seat, when
the actors dissolved
from their present ages
back into children —
such tender faces,
so given to love —
and dissolved again
into the lonesome years
without family or community,
without spouse or friend,
and then later, solitary
with spouse or friend,
and suddenly everyone
was ancient and infirm,
alone in a house
or hospital ward,
so much taken
from their eyes, their hands,
and still so given to love
I could feel the welling

of the unendurable —
but then the pale hair
darkened, the crosshatched
lines began to disappear,
and here came the same
incessant loop:
attraction and confidence
and ardor and comfort
and abandon and bliss
and control and deception
and the reckless disregard
that engenders bitterness —
until I had to leap
from my psyche-seat
into a day I needed
to embody — beyond
right and wrong,
benevolent, generous —
a day already begun
without me.

THE CHAIR

Day and night it waits for you,
simple cane-backed chair
on a stone floor, in the cool
basement of your favorite
bookstore. This is where
you settle, and turn
from one page to another,
and learn whatever
you've needed to learn:
that we are not here
all that long, that we
need one another in ways
not always negotiable,
subject to untold agonies —
and that there is a path through
this vale of self-affliction,
and it welcomes every creature
of habit and hope, who fears
that nothing's perfectible:
Thus the smile of recognition.
Thus the tears.

What Helped

What helped was also what hurt.
So many others reciting by heart
their version of the same grief.
Saying that whatever brought them
to life, to their reason for being,
would change sooner or later —
and not, it seemed, for the better.
That while they were busy
manifesting their little destinies —
punching the clock, pushing
the stroller, talking and listening
and picking up the check,
while they were trancing along

through the morning commute
and the evening commute, through
a playground, monitored hall,
prison yard, barnyard, box canyon,
through a conference call, bedroom,
waiting room, supermarket, guided orbit,
raucous arena, party of two, through
a studio of inspired chaos, along a strip
of grass, dirt, concrete, asphalt, or sand
where they took their difficult thoughts
and looked for a way out, a way in —
that while they were intent
on bettering their lots, even believed
it was already happening, if only
by the subtlest degrees —

failure was always
one step behind
and one step ahead, running
rampant through the streets

like a cheap drug, available to anyone
lacking the insight and discipline
to resist. Failure whose motto was
"Divide and conquer," that insinuated
into every heartfelt conversation
the silent vows of separation...
What helped was the story of hurt
the whole world was telling me.
Whose rueful tone was no different
from my own. Whose fitful sentences —
that would sputter and vanish
on the torturous way
to resolution — I was only
too happy to finish.

All week I moved through weather
and let weather move
through me. It didn't matter
if I was pouring tea
for a friend in some funky
hole-in-the-wall
while reciting my latest
chronology of woe,
or walking peaceably
through a day of errands, each one
a satisfaction in its completion —
water came to me from a shifting
system, whether high
in the air or in my opening
eyes. And though I didn't
count on it to come out,
the sun returned, honorable
as always, over the shameless
corporations, the deserted
playgrounds. I was nameless again,
a stranger others passed in the street
without interest, much less longing,
and more familiar to myself than ever.
No question: time was
of the essence, but so was this
no-time. It wasn't
a matter of wanting
world and more world,
but being a world: to have
in me a lone cypress
sprung from a seacliff rock,
or a cedar of Lebanon
fragrant as a loved one's hair,

the sun come back, the cold front
vanquished, the small-breasted
songbirds given to fear,
less given, chittering.

THE ROOM

A small hutch. A love seat.
An African palm whose spiky fronds
seem too much for its skinny rope of a trunk
but are not. A wall calendar, the days numbered
large and green. Tall windows on a garden.
And beyond: the shadow of the valley below.

The mantelpiece doubles as an altar:
incense, fresh flowers, the saintly figurines
and their mild salutary smiles.
And opposite, on the adjustable bed,
a congregation of one, sometimes two,
watching a movie or the news, or worshiping
music — a high fidelity for the faithful —
or by paper-shaded lamplight
reading silently or being read to.

No one mentions "vigil,"
though it might look that way.
No one says, "the dying room"
and for good reason: the Matisse
odalisque in her Turkish silks;
the beloved upright, still in tune;
the eight-legged wonder
descending on its invisible thread —
nothing that can be distinguished
from a living room.

Since when did angels start taking showers
then buses, manifesting their damp tendrils
down the aisle, a fragrance like late May flowers
in the January air? Since when did the angelic orders
start wearing hand-tooled leather boots
and warming up to the surly likes of Baudelaire?
And why shouldn't I keep to my own book
where the headstrong characters have pulled up roots
from a life so artless it's unredeemed by despair
and its sexier twin, hope? I won't look
at those fingers combing out those curls,
or that wicked curve of brow, or the slope
of forehead smooth as virgin snow.
In my book the dead still haunt the living
with promise (unfulfilled) and promises (broken),
and the living would give anything to know
what it takes to resist the token
enticements of the dead. If this isn't enough,
a crazy guy who lives near a friend of mine
climbs on with a bulging duffel bag, a paranoid
who railed at his neighbors until they got tough
and went to court. Now he's not even permitted
to leave his house, as if isolation could null-and-void
aberration, as if his threatened neighbors have outwitted
their own fears. My friend's had her run-ins with him —
she came home from work the day of a heat wave
and found him asleep at her kitchen table
in his underwear, his notorious rant and rave
reduced to a mild snore — but she's unable
or unwilling to give him up for dead.
She's bought him groceries, made some calls
to see if he can get the help he needs.
But when he hoists his big bag over a shoulder
and I see for a second a graverobber's head

swiveling toward the empty seat behind me,
I sink deeper into my book, into a colder
country where his empty eyes can't find me.

It's funny then, when I glance up again,
that he's smaller than I thought, slinking
toward his seat as if to be invisible —
until he spots the pride of the seraphim
and stops with a look that's almost risible,
and whispers to the vision across from him,
La Divina, che bellissima — as if speaking my mind:
the music, the message, the unthinking daze
that guides him straight to the source
of what he believes will sustain him
and deserves his praise. Whatever grim force
will arrest him again, then arraign him,
a dispassionate attempt to end his errant ways,
he won't be denied his *ekstasis*. Let blindness
afflict the figure of Justice. This angel brings
her human hand to his, and softly sings
her *Grazie*. There is no law greater than kindness.

THE BLUE FLAME

Another day forcing me into place:
the sun stunning, the courtyard at noon
some circle of hell strangely serene.
Neighbors off to school, to work,
even the women who already have hung on a rope
wet whites, magentas, and aquamarines.
No resolutions to speak of, no release come easy
like a break in the weather. But no ugly fights either,
no shrieking recriminations to bring the police.
Cobwebs on the cactus, on the agave and its secret
intoxication, on the endless yawn of the mouse
in deep decomposition. Hour after hour, a potent stillness
upon which nothing that is not essential
can intrude. Like that drive through the Sonora
in murderous midsummer. The pickup nicknamed
The Blue Flame — no a/c, just a steady combustion
through heat that suggested you sit still, breathe
slowly, and keep your mouth shut. Monumental
space, impervious to human foolishness,
where even the utility towers, massive as they were,
looked like little Hopi dancers frozen in place.
No telling how far I had to go or how hard it would be,
but terrain that austere reinforced the belief
I was here for the duration. Not always easy, though,
telling the ghost towns from the live ones. It took
only seconds to pass through and often no one in sight.
At most, a cowboy hat at a gas pump. And once:
a Navajo girl in black braids, dragging on a long string
a dusty pair of tennis shoes. Then the highway again,
a strict line forward through a billion years
in which life answered to no one but itself,
in which no man or woman ruined the earth
for each other. No water for miles, nothing
to cultivate, the power lines at a far remove...

And then, set back from the interstate
at the foot of a butte: a small house, turquoise,
astonishing as a mirage that won't disappear.
The sheer fact was: somebody lived here.
Somebody who managed every day
not to die. Mile after mile I wondered how
and who. And never once asked why.

VIEW #37: OCEAN BEACH

summer light lavish this late in the day

at least one bright thing
still very much in evidence

never my favorite beach   too big and available
too conspicuous   but look at how
all these people in their vehicles

have lined up facing west
as devotees face the direction
of their devotion

amateur
oceanographers   mariners   heliologists

amateur because they are here
merely (merely)
for the love of it

unlike me
who is here courtesy of "the old drearies"
here to "cut off the mind road"

and what better place than where
no roads can go

each big wave
scintillating as though
it will never end

comes to shore or rock or pier
with thunderous authority
all booming assertion   never a doubt   almost
insouciant

and is then
                shattered
                        dispersed

recombined   returned

to the beginning
of a tireless cycle

what a simple present
the present is   no elaborate
wrapping   no intricate bows

let the dust on the windshield
diffuse the light   let the light wash
all over the view   let it bathe let it lave
even the water itself

soon enough the tired
eyes will close   soon enough

they'll open again

NAIL

It was lying on the sidewalk
in front of my house, almost
invisible. A ghost of a nail,
between lives, resting. Done
with messiahs and martyrs,
the fakir's bed of cheap tricks,
the indigent dead's box of pine —
but still sleek, still sharp,
ready soon to be propelled
into a useful place.
Who knew what strength
it still might contribute,
slender though it was,
what remarkable architecture
or standard of living
it might help to begin,
complete, endure?

Once I had it in hand
I could see how it was
mottled, camouflaged
with something dark
and indeterminate —
paint or tar
or who knows what —
and for a moment
I thought of keeping it,
finding a place
on the mantelpiece
among all the other holy
objects of the ordinary
and not so ordinary.

By the time I had reached
the garbage bin, I was ready
to make of it an offering
to the god of oblivion: for me
it had fulfilled its destiny,
had delivered its timely
elemental reminder.
No doubt on another day
I would have ignored it,
another thing not worth my time.
Or I would have stepped
carelessly all over it,
like any of the purblind
hurrying from pain
to pain, fraught with defeat
and a new stratagem,
more concerned with
how much had gone wrong,
and could still go wrong,
than with what was right
in front of them.

A day as hot as my uncle's three hearths
giving rise to thirty loaves of Italian dough.
A day for white clothes and dark glasses,
for walking down the hill to lunch
with a friend I hadn't seen, it seemed,
since the sixteenth century. I passed the cyclone fences
where sweaty petals of bok choy dried, followed
the strip of shadow laid out along the edges
of each high-rise. Followed a woman with slippers
and a mouth full of gold, who kept turning around
for her little one, a girl in a bright-as-the-sun
summer dress, bent over to catch her getaway pet.
She'd snatch her grasshopper prey and play
peekaboo — until her captive leaped
to an uncertain freedom — and the whole scene
would repeat, as though to please an exacting
director. Where did she get a grasshopper anyway?
Her skin as white, her mouth as small and red
as a courtesan's in a Japanese woodblock print,
though it would be years before the spun silk
of her kimono, grasshopper-green, curved artfully
from her long neck to just under the unbitten
berry of a nipple. Years before she'd announce,
in a voice soft and level, that she didn't care
to hear her nipples compared to berries, her smile
hard as porcelain. I passed my fellow pilgrims
and reached the little park with its towering cathedral,
Dante's *Paradiso* quoted in stone: something about
God as the Great Mover, the force that brings us
to who we are. How it penetrates the universe.
The resplendence of that. Or maybe not —
my half-baked Italian the product of being
a half-breed. Then good words with an old friend
over roast eggplant on focaccia, and later chocolate gelato,

words the way they used to be: not a spell for enchantment
or miraculous conversion, or even a welcome diversion,
but good directions through a difficult landscape.
Then back up the hill in the heat, stopping here and there
for a few essentials. In a grocery bag thin and pink
as a membrane between two worlds: a soft mango
whose skin was a preview of the sunset; two apples,
half-red, half-green, named after a sacred mountain;
and a sourdough loaf, round as a life, waiting
to be torn open, to be greedily eaten.

CALLING

Remember hiking home when the bourbon sun
was maybe three fingers above the horizon —
you were hauling a paper sack of groceries —
and someone called out to you, it came
from across the street, but you didn't know
where at first? Then you saw where:
the woman lifting a white shade
behind her black iron bars. Remember how
your crossing the street, from shade
to sun, made your shadow long,
and you were glad to retrieve
the little pink spoon the woman's daughter
had dropped in the street — and the woman
grateful but the young girl caught somewhere
between scrutiny and wonderment?
Later, putting away the red pears
and the provolone, a white onion,
a sunburst squash — everything with a name
and a place to which it belonged —
you realized why you'd been convinced
you were invisible: you lived outside
your time. Your era was not inconsequential
but your name seemed to be. And yet
walking around without a substantial name —
as you did, nakedly, in a city you called
your home — you could still be given a respite
from this peculiar disembodiment.
No evidence indicated you were ready
for the award committee of posterity,
a monument erected to your best attributes,
every good wish and uncorrupted
felicity coming back to you. Not for you
the adoring millions, nor the hundreds,
not even the mailman repeating your name

as if it were a mantra or a patron saint's.
And yet you could be called by someone
in need, whom you might never see again,
or who might fail to remember you —
fail to give you your due — you could be called
and you would choose, almost
without thinking, to answer.

SOLAR

On a gray day, when the sun
has been abducted, and it's chill
end-of-the-world weather,
I must be the sun.
I must be the one
to encourage the young
sidetracked physicist
working his father's cash register
to come up with a law of nature
that says brain waves can change
the dismal sky. I must be the one
to remind the ginger plant
not to rest on the reputation
of its pungent roots, but to unveil
those buttery tendrils from the other world.
When the sky is an iron lid
I must be the one to simmer
in the piquant juices of possibility,
though the ingredients are unknown
and the day begins with a yawn.
I must issue forth a warmth
without discrimination, and any guarantee
it will come back to me.
On a dark day I must be willing
to keep my disposition light,
I have to be at the very least
one stray intact ray
of local energy, one small
but critical fraction
of illumination. Even on a day
that doesn't look gray
but still lacks comfort or sense,

I have to be the sun,
I have to shine as if
sorry life itself depended on it.
I have to make all the difference.

A WISH

I wanted to give you something for your pain.
But not the drug du jour
or the kind word this side of cliché.
Something you wouldn't find on a talk show,
in a department store or dark alleyway.
I wanted to give you something for your pain

but I couldn't imagine what.
Frankincense, myrrh — even gold
seemed too plain (too plain and too gross).
I needed something that wouldn't have occurred
to you or me, or even Nature: a creature
more fabulous, more imaginary

than you'd find in a rain forest or tapestry
or pixel-loaded screen. Some exotic anodyne
an alchemist or astrophysicist
would be envious of: a chemical reaction,
an astral refraction, an out-of-body,
out-of-mind, one-of-a-kind

transport from your pain, that would last
longer than a day, go deeper than the past.
I would have founded a whole new religion
if I thought that would suffice.
As for love — sacred, profane, or both —
I wanted to give you something

that didn't arrive with a roll of the dice
and was hard to maintain and had a knack
for disappointing. I wanted to give you
something for your pain that didn't smack
of a sorcerer's trick, or a poet's swoon,
or a psychiatrist's quip. Nothing too heavy

or spacey or glib. I'd have given you the moon
but it's been done (and besides, its desolate dust
and relentless tendency to wane
might have only exacerbated your pain).
If I could have given you something
you could depend on, could always trust

without a second thought, I would have.
A splendid view, perhaps, or a strain
of music. A favorite dish. A familiar tree.
A visit from a genie who, in lieu of granting you
a wish, would tend subtly to your every need,
and never once tire, never complain.

But when all was said and done
(or hardly said, not nearly done)
I was as helpless as you. Could you tell —
or were you so overcome your pain was all
that mattered? It seemed to me we were a kind
of kin: willing the mind its bold suspensions,

but the heart, once shattered, never quite matching
its old dimensions. And yet you persevered
in spite of pain, you knew to hold hope
as lightly as you held my hand (a phantom grasp,
a clasp that seemed to come from the other side).
And your genial smile made it plain: you were pleased
by my wish to please. And then you died.

MENTOR

for Denise Levertov

Loved your musical cackle
though you loathed the telephone.
Of course you were right: the voice alone,
even clear of static, is no substitute
for the body and its articulate beauty,
no compensation for presence,
however problematic.

Loved the winsome spirit in you
that would manifest at will
around a restaurant table, or in bed
with only your books, encouraging
the sometime reveler to revel even more
at the wicked pun, the welcome
face suddenly at the front door.

Loved how ravenous you were
for the world at large. Sidewalk
traveler, bramble-sampler,
habitué of the companionable
lake and park, taking stock of both
bloom and thorn, cloud and rock,
the heron like a white question mark.

And if there was pain (and there is
always pain) there was also the pear tree
in sun and rain, and the four
tall poplars on the lakeshore,
and so many letters from the world at large
they outnumbered the migratory flocks
(the postman begged you for a second mailbox).

I followed you as you followed
the old ones toward the sea, braced
by their lucid acuity, even as the light
began to fail, confidence gone astray.
Like you, I took the true path to be
half fog, half rumor beneath my feet.
Like you, I kept going anyway.

Chopin Laughing at Me from Deep inside Mazurka no. 13

At first it's difficult to believe
he is laughing out of anything
but *Zal,* which is a strain
of Polish bittersweetness —
at times more bitter than sweet,
not without rancor, not without tenderness —
Chopin's signature, and for which we need
no other interpreter. At first, after hours
of my struggling to decipher his notation —
at twelve I'd given up scales and grace notes
for batting practice and double plays —
trying to match his winding chromatics
with my memory of the ache of his melody,
my ear long aligned with his but not yet my fingers —
tentative, as if they were touching someone
I had lost to forces beyond my control
and who now was slowly returning to me, the tension
of touching again as if for the first time,
afraid one wrong move would dispel
whatever delicate, entrancing rhythm
had been building between us — after ages
of progress and mistake, progress and mistake, trying
to decode the cipher of his clustered loneliness,
wanting access to the gorgeous devastation —
Liszt called it "a regret borne with resignation
and without a murmur" — knowing I had to go
slowly, that was crucial (suffering and beauty
sharing the same tempo) — after many hours
of my own loneliness wanting in,
the Master relents: not only his intervals that fall
into place, like tumblers in some impregnable vault,
but each of his rests as well — a space

not really empty, a pause not so much respite
as a kind of sigh, the slow drawing in of breath as if
he were prescient, foretelling all that would come
to drain him, all the little windows in his lungs
locked shut, the blood that would rise
instead of a lilting hum to fill his throat.
And the fingering that would forego
virtuosity: the setbacks to come, his
irreplaceable losses, lending themselves
not to a humiliating diminuendo of powers
but to simplicity: a new form of mastery...
After hours of wanting to play the way
he could, hold the gift he'd been born
to give, and give it away, or rather let it be
taken — to honor your daunting life,
your beautiful purpose, your passions
even as they pass from you — which is
what music is, the audible interplay
between presence and absence —
after hours of my fumbling and frustration
he lets me join him. And I swear I hear him
laughing: *piano,* softly, not
out of "desperate gaiety,"
as one commentator says,
and not out of the bitterness
of having to leave the world too early,
while someone as imperfect as I should still be alive
to dim and smudge his brilliance
if not entirely snuff it out —
but laughing because I came to him
with a familiar desperation, because
he knew me to be a countryman

from the realm of Love If You Can
Whatever Is Still Alive, Though Imperfect,
because I knew the way in would be arduous
but worth my patience, laughing at me
because I did not give up.

I'm Walking down the Street,
Minding My Own Business

chitchatting with my ebullient consort, peach of a summer afternoon —
when a man comes toward us in the crosswalk,
a fat Cheshire grin in a blue hospital gown —
"Here comes your next boyfriend," I say, just before two dark blue
uniforms hurry up behind him, turn him around.

I'm walking down the street, minding my own business,
when strung out before me on the sidewalk
are sixteen slices of bread (looks like whole wheat):
Hansel and Gretel have grown so old
their eyesight isn't what it used to be.

I'm walking down the street, minding my own business,
when a woman in blue jeans two sizes too big
pulls them down, panties and all, and hunkers
in front of my house, and takes a humongous dump,
and when I pretend not to notice but am still muttering
an invective against the absent powers that be, she says to me,
"You wouldn't happen to have any toilet paper handy, would you?"

I'm walking down the street, minding my own business,
which amounts to little more than considering my sorry-ass
state of penury, when — is that actual paper money
swirling in the gust over my head? And then the din
of all these people at the next intersection — I mean *in*
the intersection — old folks and whippersnappers and
punks and suits — they're grabbing up what I find out later
is the jettisoned loot from an aborted bank robbery
(some of the money bags contained an exploding red dye
planted by the bank for such an occasion), and here comes
a tumblin' tumbleweed of twenty-dollar bills, followed by
a phalanx of squealing schoolkids, who seem to have just discovered
the manic wonders of adrenaline, followed by a white-haired gent

in tam-o'-shanter and windbreaker, who bends to each bill at his feet
with... such... snail... slowness... the wind snatches it away before he can —
and I'm so stunned by the whole commotion I do nothing at all
to improve the ruinous fiscal year — but find out later the schoolkids
returned all the money anyway, even the perfectly clean cash,
and that the only loot still missing was taken by some middle-aged woman
seen leaping out of a green Mercedes, stuffing an oversized handbag
from Bottega Veneta, and whisking away like the larcenous wind...

I'm walking down the street, minding my own business,
and a woman I once came this close to falling for
is unloading groceries from her car with her kid,
and she says this morning she remembered the night
she sat on my couch, and I asked her if she'd remove
from her piled-up hair the chopstick of black lacquer —
the inlaid mother-of-pearl had been flirting with the August moonlight —
and she did... And she smiles with more pleasure than not
when she says she has been carrying that moment
all through her day, and I smile too when I walk away.

I'm walking down the street, minding my own business,
passing others minding their own business, and no one
looks at anyone, or makes a sound, no one says a word.

So I'm walking down the street, minding my own business —
because walking down the street *is* my business, I'm a
professional perambulator, vagabond, itinerant, man-about-town,
Mr. Peripatetic, traveling incognito, a classical air for accompaniment
or a walking blues, no need to heed the official signs —
STOP, YIELD, DO NOT ENTER, NOT A THROUGH STREET —
sometimes only my shadow for a consort, sometimes
only the insistent wind, we two wending our way in and out,
up and down, over and under and through, toward some remarkable
whatever — maybe, just maybe, toward you.

SPLENDOR

One day it's the clouds,
one day the mountains.
One day the latest bloom
of roses — the pure monochromes,
the dazzling hybrids — inspiration
for the cathedral's round windows.
Every now and then
there's the splendor
of thought: the singular
idea and its brilliant retinue —
words, cadence, point of view,
little gold arrows flitting
between the lines.
And too the splendor
of no thought at all:
hands lying calmly
in the lap, or swinging
a six iron with effortless
tempo. More often than not
splendor is the star we orbit
without a second thought,
especially as it arrives
and departs. One day
it's the blue glassy bay,
one day the night
and its array of jewels,
visible and invisible.
Sometimes it's the warm clarity
of a face that finds your face
and doesn't turn away.
Sometimes a kindness, unexpected,
that will radiate farther
than you might imagine.
One day it's the entire day

itself, each hour foregoing
its number and name,
its cumbersome clothes, a day
that says come as you are,
large enough for fear and doubt,
with room to spare: the most secret
wish, the deepest, the darkest,
turned inside out.

At the Asian Art Museum

Turtles on pond rock,
sculptures we admire —
till one of them moves

❧

Turtle lifts his face
to the sun — one hundred years
of working on his tan

❧

Who has more beauty —
Buddha with perfect gold leaf
or Buddha with none

❧

How long I've sat here,
alone, forgetting myself
and being reminded

❧

Leaving the galleries,
no more portraits, likenesses —
just one cherry tree

SOME LITTLE HAPPINESS

knows our names
and where we live
and sets out to meet us halfway.

It arrives humming,
an enchantment of tones
we have never heard
and don't want to let go,
because we know
they will never be heard again.

Some little happiness lives
in our eyes, in our skin,
leaves a trace in the lines
around our tired mouths.

Some little happiness.

We don't have to deserve it,
we don't have to expect it,
we don't even have to admit
how much we need it,

and some little happiness
will rest its hand on our hands,
will tell us, Take me,
I won't be here that long,
and neither will you.

It's okay, whispers
some little happiness,
trust me.

And we do.

It was just last week. The leafy plaza at the entrance to Berkeley's campus. Warm sun for my 30th birthday. I liked turning 30, a nice round even number, my turbulent 20s behind me at last. There was no place in particular I had to be just yet, and it was lovely to watch a young woman with a long thick braid fling a plastic disk for her leaping Akita. Both the disk and the dog were white and looked as if they might have been beamed down from another star cluster. The woman, though, was all Earth: freckled cheekbones, tie-dyed T-shirt, faded cutoffs. Long legs, subtly muscled, which flexed and balanced on bare feet. I imagined that long braid undone, how it would fan across a pillowcase. I wasn't in love with her but thought of how little it would take. A thought which, now that I was 30, both tickled and chastened me. Suddenly here comes a tweedy professor-type, imperious eyebrows, brown valise, his stride rhythmical and purposeful. On a faculty of Nobel laureates he is one of the most celebrated, a poet renowned for wrestling with the tenacious angels of politics and religion and identity. His sudden appearance makes me question if I should curtail the chasing of skirts (or soft well-worn denim shorts), putting them behind me with other so-called childish things, and replace them with loftier aspirations toward which I might apply my own vigorous and purposeful strides. Mr. Nobel looks as though he has learned to be in the world but not of it, and at 30, while I have no firsthand knowledge of a tank turning a street corner, or the rigorous benefits of Saint Benedict's Rule, I am intimate with self-regard, a two-way mirror whereby I am often confronted with my own reflection, flawed and dismaying, but sometimes find myself on the other side as well, leaning back in a chair, my fingers linked in my lap, while I observe with dispassion the perpetrator of self-absorption facing me, my benighted twin, who occasionally suspects he is a subject of scrutiny by the powers that be.

Mr. Nobel strides by, the barefoot beauty flings a disk her alien dog snatches with a flash of teeth, I think, "I am 30, I am 30," and now it is this week and I am 46, and I recall that Mr. Nobel is the same man who once described his lover's genitalia as her "velvet yoni," the same man who despaired over a dark-haired woman he had seen briefly on a train. And here is a striking woman all in black — coat, dress, stockings, shoes — walking slowly to her café table to keep her coffee from spilling. All in black, like a priestess or an assassin. Ally or enemy? Or neither — simply a confluence of needs and wounds and wonders and dreams? Black for the Unknown, the deathless theme that we do not write so much as it writes us. She sits and sips and peruses her paper and now and then smiles subtly at me. I am 46. Next week I will be 62. The week after, 78, and the week after that, who knows? It is my nature, it has always been my nature, to be in the world, and of it. And not of it.

VIEW #45

after Hokusai and Hiroshige

I dreamt half my life was spent
in wonder, and never suspected.

So immersed in the moment
I forgot I was ever there.

Red-tailed hawk turning
resistance into ecstasy.

The patrolmen joking with the drunk
whose butt seemed glued to the sidewalk.

A coral quince blossom in winter,
pink as a lover's present.

And tilting my bamboo umbrella
against the warm slant

of rain, was I not a happy peasant
crossing the great bay on a bridge that began

who knows when, and will end
who knows when?

ABOUT THE AUTHOR

Thomas Centolella has been the recipient of a Lannan Literary Fellowship, the American Book Award, and the Poetry Medal from the Commonwealth Club of California, among other honors. He lives in San Francisco and teaches throughout the Bay Area.

The Chinese character for poetry is made up of two parts: "word" and "temple." It also serves as pressmark for Copper Canyon Press.

Founded in 1972, Copper Canyon Press remains dedicated to publishing poetry exclusively, from Nobel laureates to new and emerging authors. The press thrives with the generous patronage of readers, writers, booksellers, librarians, teachers, students, and funders — everyone who shares the conviction that poetry invigorates the language and sharpens our appreciation of the world.

PUBLISHERS' CIRCLE
Allen Foundation for the Arts
Lannan Foundation
Lila Wallace–Reader's Digest Fund
National Endowment for the Arts

EDITORS' CIRCLE
Breneman Jaech Foundation
Port Townsend Paper Company
Washington State Arts Commission

For information and catalogs:

COPPER CANYON PRESS
Post Office Box 271
Port Townsend, Washington 98368
360/385-4925
poetry@coppercanyonpress.org
www.coppercanyonpress.org

Views from along the Middle Way has been set in Adobe Garamond, drawn by Robert Slimbach and based on type cut in the sixteenth century by Claude Garamond. Book design and composition by Wendy Holdman.

CPSIA information can be obtained at www.ICGtesting.com
Printed in the USA
LVOW11s0457181115

462945LV00003B/24/P

9 781556 591617